Eat at Joan's

by Frederick Prugh
illustrated by Jane McCreary

Core Decodable 84

McGraw Hill Education

Bothell, WA • Chicago, IL • Columbus, OH • New York, NY

MHEonline.com

Send all inquiries to:
McGraw-Hill Education
8787 Orion Place
Columbus, OH 43240

ISBN: 978-0-02-144883-8
MHID: 0-02-144883-3

Printed in China

11 12 13 14 15 DSS 29 28 27 26 25

My name is Joan.
I own this shop.
The shop is on the coast.

My shop is a drive-in.

Cars drive in and out.

Drivers get a meal at a value price.

I make a few yummy dishes.
I make my own veggie roast.
I make my own meatloaf.

The sun went down slowly.

I looked at the sea.

A lone boat sailed on the waves.

A gentle wind was blowing.
The sailboat was not far away.

Lots of boats have passed this way.
But few have stopped.
Why did this boat sail closer?

But I could not look.
Lots of cars were in line.
They filled the road.

I had to stay at the window.
I had to hand out dinners.
I had to do it fast.

Still I could see the boat.
It was sailing to the coast.
Then it stopped.

A rowboat left the boat.
Men rowed it to the coast.

The men talked to me.
"We need fuel," they said.

I was confused.
Sailboats do not need fuel.
Wind makes sailboats go.

But then I got it.
Fuel meant stuff to eat.
The men were hungry!

"Boat or not," I said.
"You must wait in line."
And they did.